JLA

Story by
Alex Ross and Paul Dini

Text by Paul Dini

Art by Alex Ross

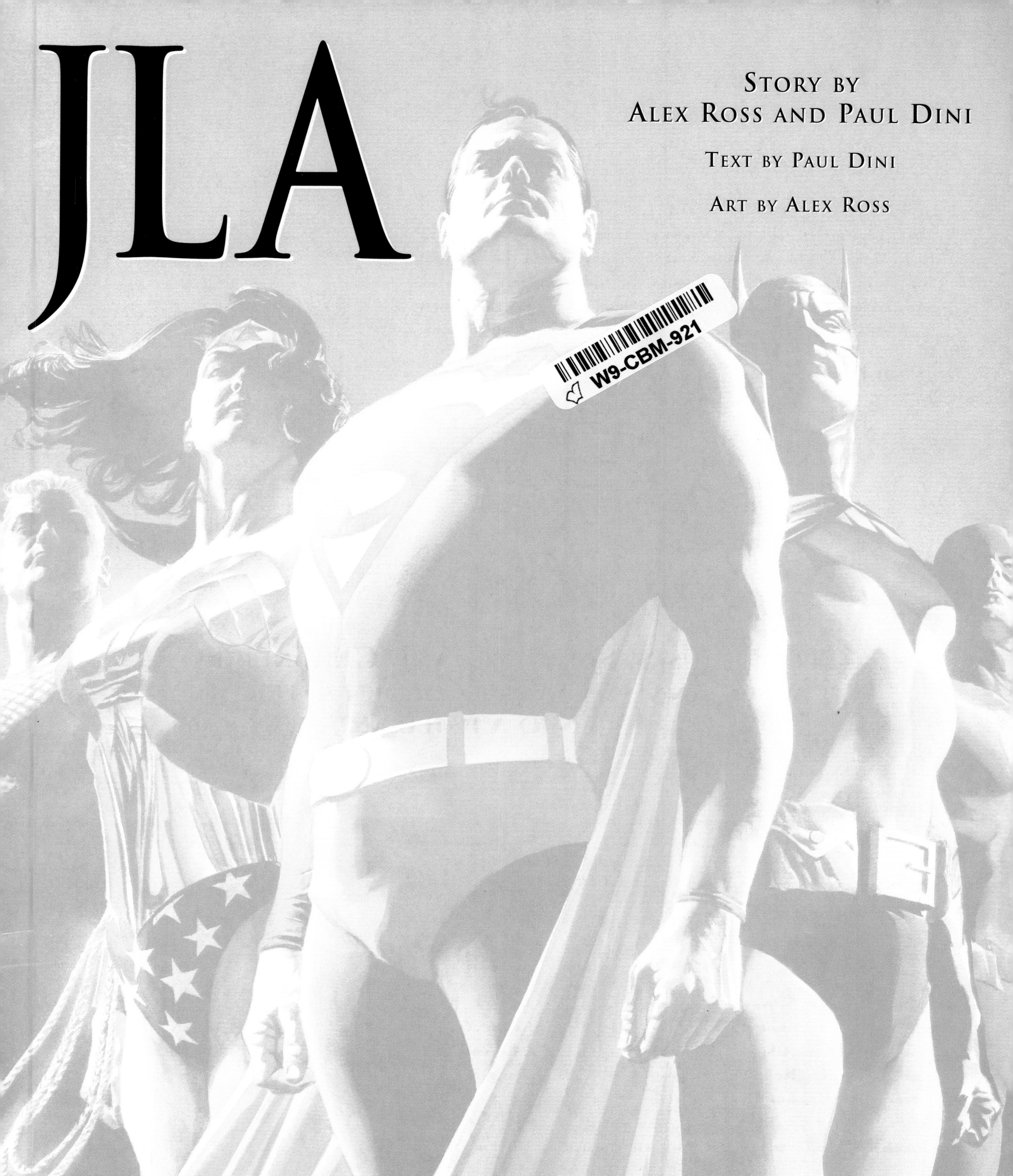

SECRET ORIGINS

My deepest thanks to Charles Kochman, Joey Cavalieri, Rich Thomas, Rob Simpson, and everyone else on the editorial and research staffs at DC Comics for furnishing me with the lore and legends of the DCU. Special thanks also to Alan Burnett for his ready ear, great inspiration, and countless good suggestions.

—Paul Dini

To Julius S. Schwartz and Gardner Fox,
who fanned a faded golden afterglow
into a brilliant silver age.

My thanks, as always, goes to my models: Frank Kasy, Matt Paoletti, Rhonda Hampton, Cory and Logan Smith, Anthony Vitale, Chris Fleming, Sal Abbinanti, Karen Kooi, Robert Miller, Keith Anderson, Scott Beaderstadt, Rachel Silverman, Clark and T.J. Ross.

Thanks also to Teresa Vitale and Leeman Yuen for costume help.

—Alex Ross

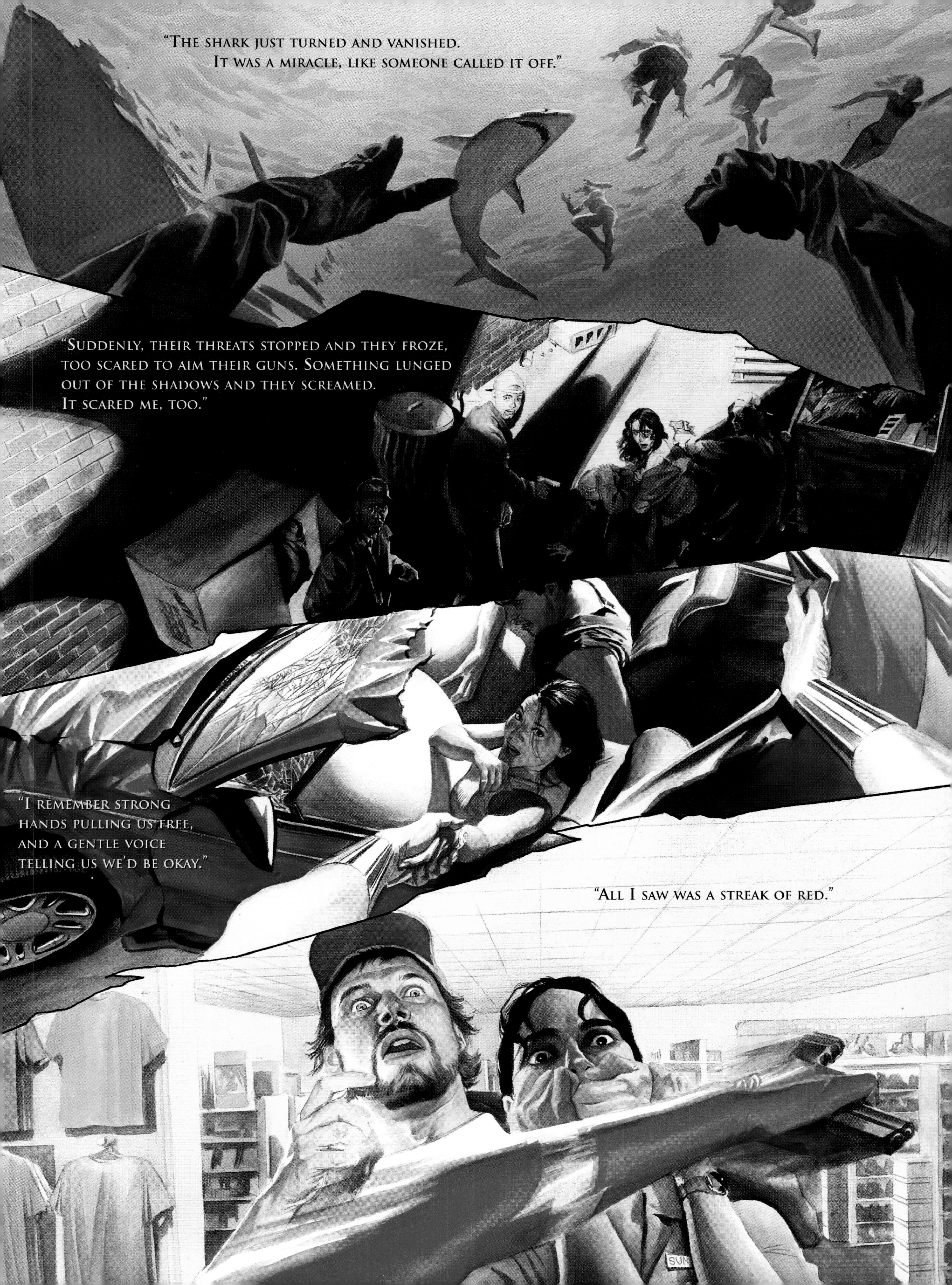
"The shark just turned and vanished. It was a miracle, like someone called it off."
"Suddenly, their threats stopped and they froze, too scared to aim their guns. Something lunged out of the shadows and they screamed. It scared me, too."
"I remember strong hands pulling us free, and a gentle voice telling us we'd be okay."
"All I saw was a streak of red."

They are heroes who act during life's darkest moments. Sometimes unseen...
Sometimes coloring the skies with their amazing feats.
Warriors, protectors, guardian angels.

They are beings of great power and greater commitment, working miracles for all mankind.
And sheltering us when the sky is falling.

THE PLANET KRYPTON WAS DOOMED.
JUST BEFORE ITS DESTRUCTION, A SCIENTIST PLACED HIS ONLY SON IN A SMALL ROCKET AND SENT HIM TO SAFETY.
I WAS THAT CHILD.
THE ROCKET LANDED ON EARTH. . .
WHERE I WAS FOUND BY A KINDLY COUPLE, THE KENTS.
THEY NAMED ME CLARK AND RAISED ME AS THEIR OWN.
EVEN AS A BOY, I KNEW I WAS DIFFERENT FROM EVERYONE AROUND ME.
THROUGH THEIR LOVE AND GUIDANCE, MY ADOPTIVE PARENTS TAUGHT ME TO USE AND UNDERSTAND MY SPECIAL GIFTS.
AS I GREW OLDER, I DISCOVERED. . .
I COULD DEFY GRAVITY.

I could run faster
than anything
created by man.
My strength
was tremendous and
my body invulnerable
to harm.
I later became a
reporter, able to
walk among men
and be nearby
when needed.
In times of trouble,
I am there as. . .
SUPERMAN
To fight for liberty and justice,
I have sworn to protect the
world that has taken this child
of Krypton and embraced him
as one of her own.

I AM THE
BATMAN
A GRIM SOUL FIGHTING A RELENTLESS WAR ON CRIME.
CLOAKED IN SHADOWS, I PREY ON THE FORCES OF EVIL.
DETERMINED TO STRIKE TERROR THROUGHOUT THE UNDERWORLD, I ADOPTED THE FEARSOME IMAGE OF A BAT.
TO PREPARE MYSELF FOR THE BATTLE, I DEVELOPED MY MIND, MASTERING SCIENCE AND CRIMINOLOGY.
I PUSHED MYSELF TO THE LIMITS OF HUMAN ENDURANCE, TRAINING MY BODY TO PHYSICAL PERFECTION...

All the while driven by the pain of my worst memory—
The night a criminal stepped from the shadows and tore my world apart.
In a heartbeat I had lost the two most important people in my life.
It was this loss that changed me forever...
The night a grief-stricken boy made a solemn oath he would never forget.

Since the time of our creation at the hands of the gods, we Amazons have had to struggle for our place in man's often savage world.
Weary of constant warfare, we beseeched our patron goddess for a sanctuary. The will of gentle Aphrodite guided us away from the battlefields to the shores of Paradise Island.
Now free to develop our minds as well as our bodies, we created Themyscira, a refuge of spiritual and intellectual tranquility, with technological advances that far surpassed those of the mortal world.
But Aphrodite's greatest gift was the ability granted to me, Hippolyta. As Amazon ruler, I created a living daughter out of the Earth itself. I named her Diana. For years she lived and grew as the beloved princess of our nation.
Over time, we had grown out of touch with the rest of humankind. The outside world could benefit from our knowledge, but any ambassador would surely face distrust.
It would be a mission that would tax the stamina of the greatest Amazon, if such a worthy one could be found. A tournament was held.

A mysterious champion emerged—a woman strong enough in body and spirit to meet the challenges before her.
To my surprise and sorrow it was Diana. She could have remained safely within our realm, but my willful daughter was determined to take on this frustrating and thankless task. Her choice was made.
Diana was now
WONDER WOMAN
I released her into the danger and uncertainty of Man's World.
In her travels, she brings the sum total of Amazon courage and knowledge, guided by a compassionate heart toward all people in need.

You may know him as
a Scarlet Speedster called
The FLASH
But to me, Barry Allen
was always a career slowpoke.
Pragmatic and methodical, yes,
but chronically late, much to the
consternation of his long-suffering fiancée.
I swear there were times I would have throttled that man, if he ever bothered to show up on time. Like on that one stormy night.
We had a date, but Barry let the hours slip away, of course. There he sat in the police lab, working away on some bit of scientific minutiae, oblivious to the world around him.
And then, in one blinding flash, that same world became too fast for him.
I don't have to draw you a picture. I'll just say that my man suddenly discovered he could make up for all that lost time.

As a matter of fact, now he had time to burn.
To his eyes, he was a normal man in a slow-motion world. It was like he had been blessed with the speed of Mercury.
Hamburger
WITH
ONIONS
FR. FRIE
Though another legend, fondly remembered from Barry's childhood, pointed the way to the path he would take.
NO.1-JAN.
LIGHTNING FAST ACTION. MYSTER
Introducing... THE FLASH... Fastest man alive!
Yes, to the world at large, the Flash is the Fastest Man Alive. But when he's with me, Iris Allen, he still takes it slow.

GREEN LANTERN
Famed throughout the universe are the acts of heroism performed by the men and women chosen to bear this title.
From thousands upon thousands of worlds they have been summoned. Dedicated souls possessing the deepest commitment to preserving peace and galactic justice.
The Lanterns' only weapons: rings of near-limitless power that make the wearer's every command a reality.
The Guardians of Oa, beings of vast intellect, bestowed this power to me and others chosen from every galaxy, to serve them as members of the Green Lantern Corps..
I lived by the oath I swore to uphold, a promise to shine my light against the dark, against evil.
But the time came for m
to seek out a successor.

My ring was drawn to
man from Earth whose
pirit of adventure and
quest for knowledge
outstripped even my own.
A man of tremendous conviction and a passion for justice. This last deed, then, would be my legacy.
The most important mission I, Abin Sur, would ever complete.
My last deed before dying was to summon pilot Hal Jordan, and bestow my ring upon the man who would one day become the greatest Green Lantern of all.

His name is Arthur. His title is King. You know him as
AQUAMAN
The absolute ruler of two-thirds of the Earth.
His story began here, with a lone woman of noble birth on a wave-tossed raft.
A refugee from our world below, she was rescued by a lighthouse keeper. The wayward princess fell in love with her kindly savior, and he with her.
This union of Earth and sea produced a son.
A special child who bridged the gulf between those two worlds.

n time, the boy's uesting soul drove im to seek his mother's homeland—the undersea kingdom of Atlantis.
Here he grew into a hero and reclaimed the heritage that was his birthright.
So the broken circle was made whole again, as the new King began a dynasty of his own.
And who am I? Simply a legend of a child, told by the people of Atlantis, echoed among its creatures and whispered in the waves of the eternal sea.

THIS WAS A WORLD OF POETRY AND SONG, LIFE AND LOVE.

NO MORE.

THE MARS I KNEW IS NOW A PLACE AS BARREN AS IT IS LONELY.

Taking the role of a detective, I used my psychic powers to discover the truth behind seemingly unsolvable crimes.
And when necessary, employed a more formidable appearance in order to startle and subdue the real culprits.
Thus, in the manner of so many immigrants before me, I found a way to assimilate into the greater population, yet my strange heritage ensures my isolation. Though I walk among you, I am always alone.
MARTIAN MANHUNTER
With abilities beyond imagining, I fight to preserve the nobler aspirations of humankind, in the hope that my adopted home never suffers the same fate as my beloved Mars.

Yeah, I'll tell you a story.
It begins with a well-heeled punk with too much money, no ambition, and the only direction in his life being over the side of his seagoing yacht. A couple days later, he washed up on the beach with the rest of the trash. One guy surviving on a deserted island by himself? Forget the movie; it wasn't that easy. This rich boy had a choice: learn to use homemade weapons or starve.
Green Arrow
Going hungry wasn't an option, so I forced myself to master the bow and arrow. After weeks of practice, I was good. No, exceptional.
Before you call me conceited, let me assure you that going without for so long humbled me quite nicely. I only took what I needed and was grateful to have it.
The experience opened my eyes. When I finally made it home, I decided to use my skills and new attitude where they'd do the most good.
I became a sort of urban Robin Hood, a self-appointed champion of the little guy.
For a while I had a partner. A good kid, talented, brave, and no stranger to adversity himself. He conquered his personal demons and moved on. So did I.

And yeah, I did my time with the League. But ultimately, it was not the group that held my heart.
That belonged to those people down there. The ones carrying on their own fights against injustice and a world that would cast them aside.
Equal Choice
No War
It was a lonely vigil at first, but lucky for me, I met a pretty bird who felt the same way—Black Canary.
What do you know? Looks like the rich boy's finally got some direction in his life. Just never give me reason to direct it at you.

Thanagar.
A scientifically advanced world patrolled by winged peacekeepers called Hawkmen. My father, Paran Katar, invented the technology that gave the Hawks their wings.
I, Katar Hol, grew to become our world's most highly decorated officer. Then came a day when one of Thanagar's most notorious criminals fled our world for Earth.
We were quickly dispatched to make the capture—
—myself and my wife, Officer Shayera Thal. Upon completion of our mission, we decided to stay on Earth.

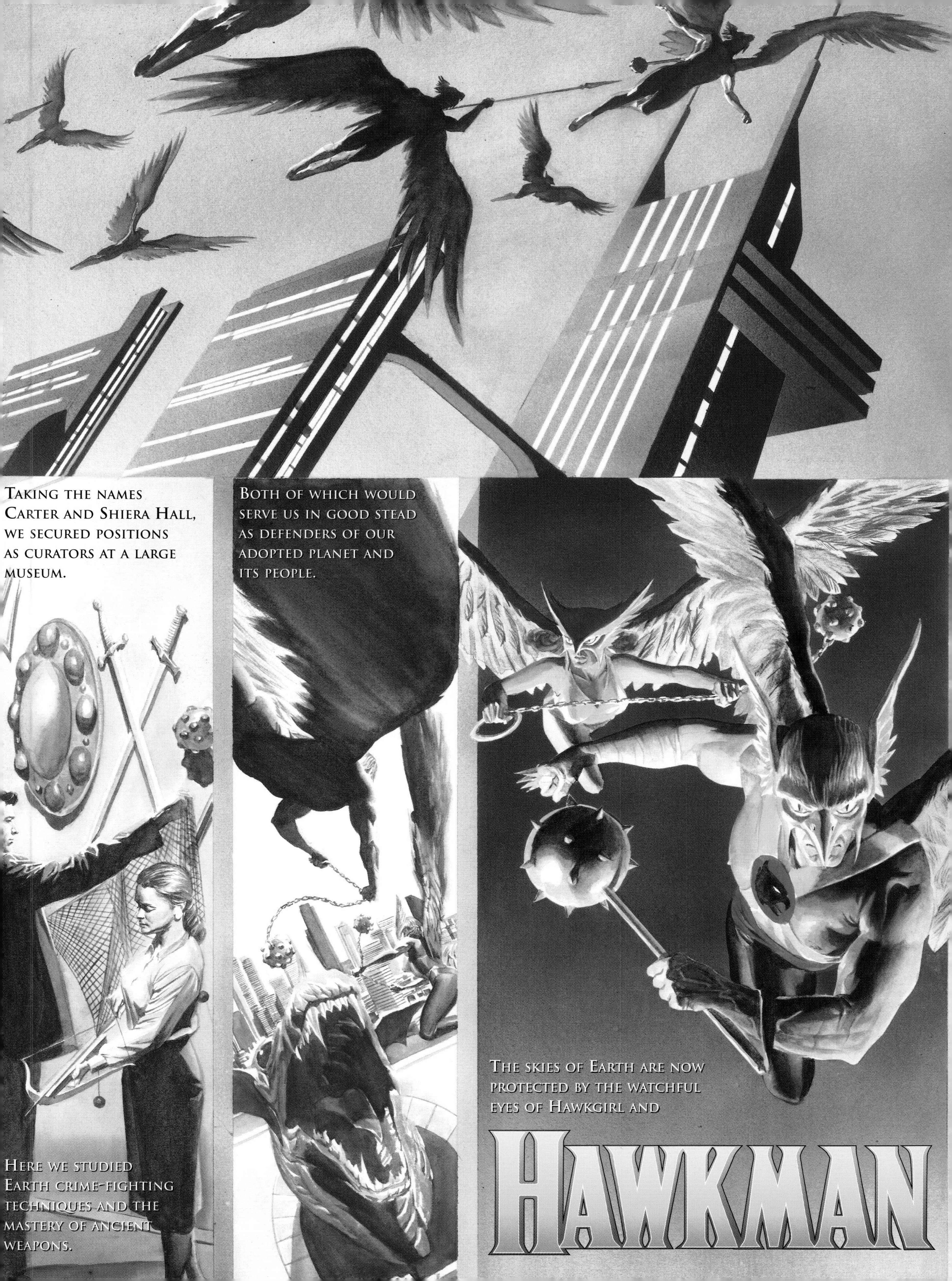

Taking the names Carter and Shiera Hall, we secured positions as curators at a large museum.
Here we studied Earth crime-fighting techniques and the mastery of ancient weapons.
Both of which would serve us in good stead as defenders of our adopted planet and its people.
The skies of Earth are now protected by the watchful eyes of Hawkgirl and
HAWKMAN

Size matters? I don't think so.
I prefer to say, "The bigger they are,
the harder they fall." It's a fitting
motto for the man who named himself
The ATOM
Looking at me now, it's hard to believe I was once the tallest guy in my class. Of course, that was before Professor Ray Palmer happened upon the remains of a falling star.
A white dwarf star, to be exact, possessing incredible density and miraculous physical properties.
I fashioned a lens from a fragment of the star, and through it focused beams of ultraviolet light.
This caused an inanimate object to shrink to a fraction of its size. One drawback—the shrinking process always destroyed the test subjects.
A unique factor in my genetic makeup allowed me to survive the shifts in size and mass. I incorporated the dwarf star material into a special costume that enabled me to change at will.

Only a small man, so to speak, would have kept this ability to himself. Therefore, I was determined to use my skills wherever they are needed. For example, I can "ride" electronic impulses through a phone wire into a criminal's lair.
Thanks to the dwarf star density, I can command the strength of a man many times my normal size.
And shrinking even smaller, I can stride like a giant across innumerable subatomic galaxies.
But my proudest achievements are those I have made as a member of a team of unique men and women who accept me with equal stature. It just goes to show you, never underestimate the little guy.

THE SEVEN D
There is an eternal battle between mankind and the dark forces that seek its destruction.
For thousands of years I used the powers of ancient gods and heroes to fight on the side of righteousness.
PRIDE
ENVY
GREED
But my time on the mortal plane grew short, and I searched for a new champion to take my place.
From a distance, I saw young Billy Batson, a good-hearted boy cast out by a cruel uncle.
But Billy persevered without complaining. Within him I sensed the worthy soul I had been seeking. I sent my mystic emissary...
SU
...who brought the boy before me.
I told Billy of the great struggle for mankind's soul.
If he accepted my offer, Billy would be granted the power to defend the poor and helpless.
He could use this gift to right wrongs and crush evil everywhere.

ADLY ENEMIES OF MAN
HATRED
SELFISHNESS
LAZINESS
INJUSTICE
FROM THE NAMES OF THE NCIENTS I HAD FASHIONED MY OWN.
"SPEAK MY NAME!"
"SHAZAM!"
SOLOMON WISDOM
HERCULES STRENGTH
ATLAS STAMINA
ZEUS POWER
ACHILLES COURAGE
MERCURY SPEED
BY INVOKING IT, THE BOY WOULD BECOME THE MIGHTIEST HERO IN THE WORLD.
AND SO WAS BORN-
Captain MARVEL

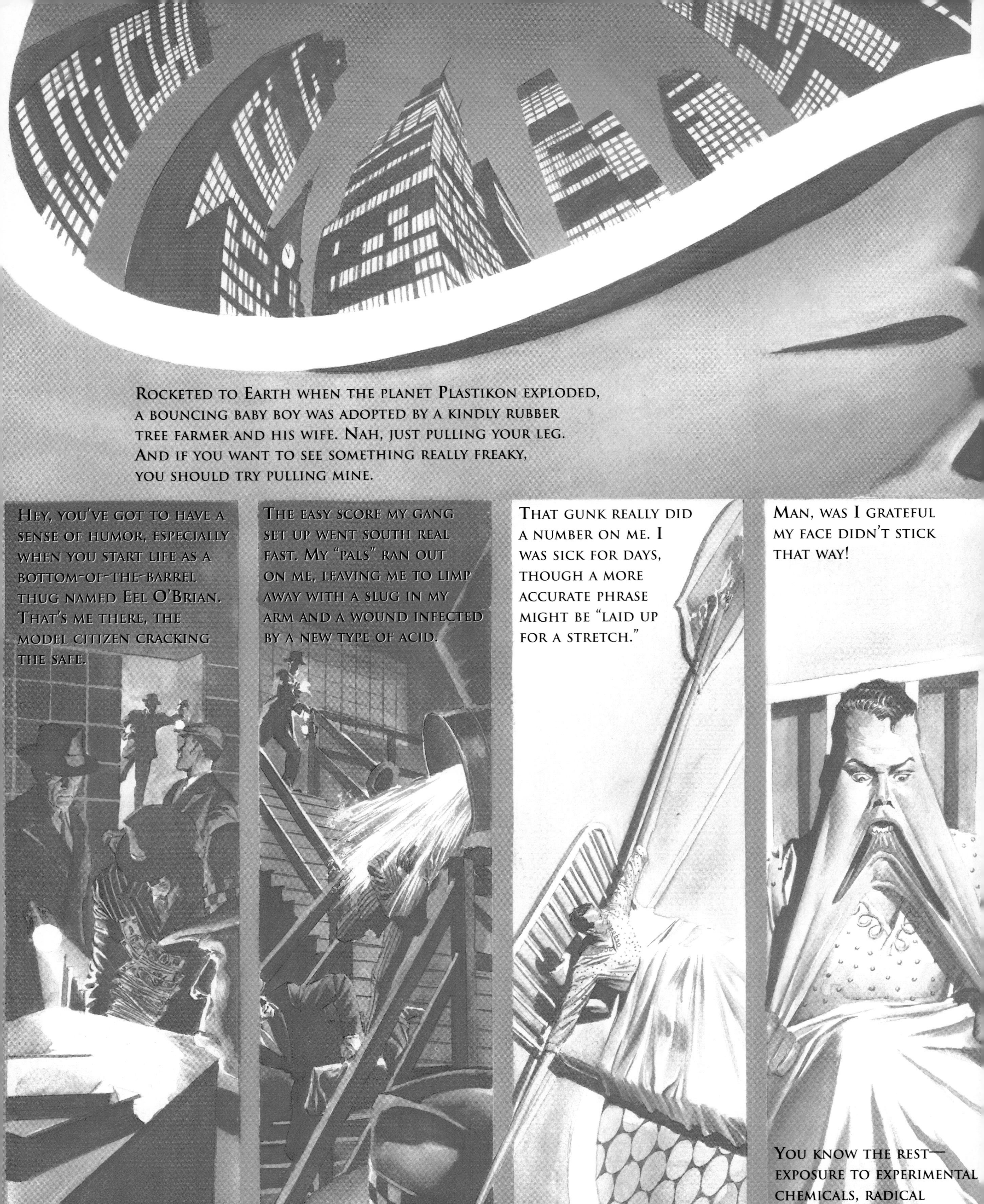

Rocketed to Earth when the planet Plastikon exploded, a bouncing baby boy was adopted by a kindly rubber tree farmer and his wife. Nah, just pulling your leg. And if you want to see something really freaky, you should try pulling mine.

But the biggest change was that I no longer needed money or power, or all the petty things that seemed so important just a few days before.
I was still serious about one thing—using my new abilities to atone for my past.
As Eel O'Brian, I set up the same kinds of rats who left me to die, then slipped into my alterable ego to take them down.
After all, it ain't easy to get over on a guy who can be anything from a lady's vanity table to the very book you're reading now.
Ha! Made you look!
PLASTIC MAN

The Flash. Aquaman. Wonder Woman. Green Lantern. Martian Manhunter. Five heroes who banded together to battle a common threat from the stars.

They were soon joined by Superman and Batman, and in time, an extended team of Earth's mightiest protectors was assembled.

Each member brings to the group the deepest commitment to preserving justice and the rights and liberties of all mankind.

Over the years, many other heroes have fought alongside the League, adding their unique abilities and powers to the cause.

The Earth-born space adventurer, Adam Strange.

Zatanna, mistress of magic and defender against dark arts.

Metamorpho, the ever-changing element man.

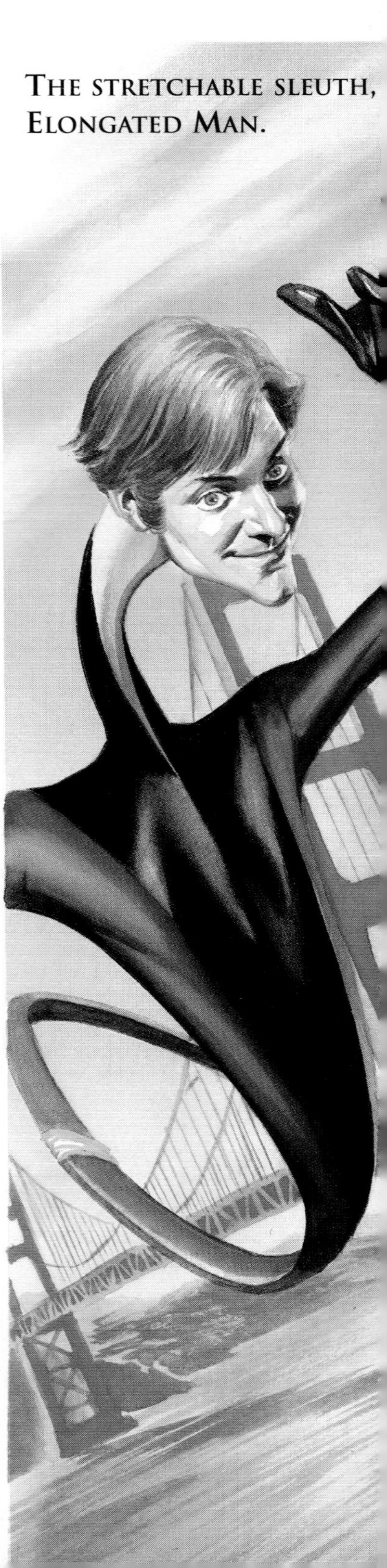

The stretchable sleuth, Elongated Man.

Phantom Stranger, enigmatic and all knowing, at one with the cosmos but forever alone.

And Earth's air elemental contained in android form, the Red Tornado.

Together they have vowed not to control humanity, but to combat the forces that threaten it.

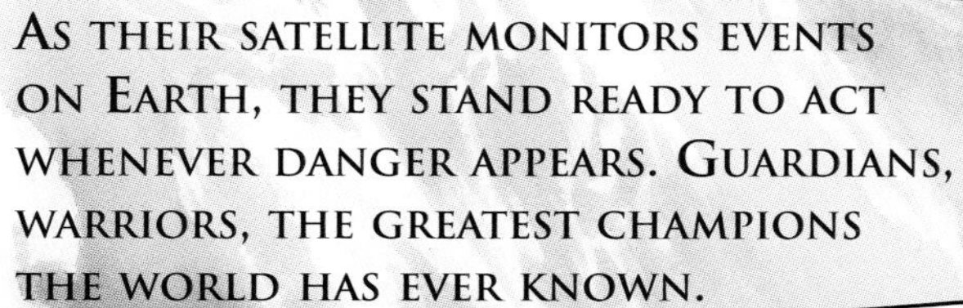

As their satellite monitors events on Earth, they stand ready to act whenever danger appears. Guardians, warriors, the greatest champions the world has ever known.

Clark Kent might find it comfortable and roomy to become Superman in a store room or an under-used office, but for the editorial team of CHARLES KOCHMAN, JOEY CAVALIERI, and RICH THOMAS, the spare, vacant office down the end of the hall made for cramped quarters. It was also as silent and somber as the Batcave, given that a power outage in the DC offices at 1700 Broadway had knocked out everybody's computers and incoming phone calls. But at least that guaranteed few interruptions: the quiet allowed them to hook up a recorder to a speakerphone, and capture the busy ALEX ROSS in his studio in Illinois. Not quite a Fortress of Solitude, but mighty close.

PAUL DINI, on the other hand, was in Philadelphia, lurking about the set of the new Kevin Smith movie *Jersey Girl*. Apparently all that time he spent writing Batman has made him adept at crashing any high-security site.

INTERVIEW WITH ALEX ROSS, WEDNESDAY, OCTOBER 2, 2002

CHARLES KOCHMAN: **All right, the tape is running, so you have to be nice.**

ALEX ROSS: Oh, dear God. [*Laughter*]

CHARLES: **So here we are, year five. Originally this series of tabloids was conceived as four stand-alone volumes on Superman, Batman, Captain Marvel, and Wonder Woman. In the past year or so, the idea of an expanded, all-star super hero adventure began to take shape: next year's JLA: LIBERTY AND JUSTICE. But what about JLA: SECRET ORIGINS? What's the "secret origin" of this project?**

ALEX: Well, I would say it came from the ideas of you and Joey. You know, we had, not a disagreement, but a discussion on the use of the new origins that were going to precede the story of LIBERTY AND JUSTICE: those of the Flash, Green Lantern, and Aquaman. The way the book was originally set up, the feeling was that it was too front-loaded with those origin spreads. There was no natural flow. Showing only those three seemed less than fully satisfactory. So, it was an invention of yours to create a side project that would essentially be a companion to that book but also stand on its own, which it certainly does. It works as a primer to all who are coming for the first time to DC's characters, wondering who these legends are. But it doesn't really make any difference if SECRET ORIGINS has a graphic novel like LIBERTY AND JUSTICE following it because the book has its own purpose.

CHARLES: **So we noticed that this book is dedicated to DC editor Julie Schwartz and writer Gardner Fox. How come?**

ALEX: Essentially, the JLA is so much an invention of the Silver Age, and the characters featured are the primary icons of that era. The Silver Age Flash, Green Lantern, Hawkman, and all the subsequent versions of older, long-running characters like Superman, Batman, Aquaman—all of them come through the filter of the new Silver Age that was heralded under the editorial influence of Julius Schwartz and the creative writing of Gardner Fox. Particularly as an editor-writer combination, these two put the most thought into recrafting DC's super heroes and ultimately creating the legends that would stand for years to follow.

CHARLES: **Which leads to quite an interesting point. In SECRET ORIGINS and LIBERTY AND JUSTICE, you have a particular lineup that you and Paul have chosen. Why that configuration of super heroes, and also why those particular versions?**

ALEX: Well, they are the most legendary, well-known forms of those characters, the ones that have lasted the longest. For the case of, say, heroes like the Flash, Green Lantern, Hawkman—these are versions that have lasted for, like, forty years before there were any revisions made to either their looks or their identities.

CHARLES: **I remember you recently said something to me about Hal Jordan's costume, that it was the same up until a few years ago for however many years, but even Kyle Rayner's costume, which is relatively recent, just changed in the last few months. There's this total state of flux.**

ALEX: Exactly. Gil Kane's design for the Hal Jordan Green Lantern is one of the most classic comic book costume designs ever. It is one of the most influential throughout comic book history. The look of that character, the definition of who that man was, all of that is such a powerful thing. This is the era that we wanted to respond to. And of course, the added fact is that it's the era both me and the other creative people working on this—Paul, the editors—this is what we grew up on. It's what we know intimately. And because there is the option to do a creative story like this, we grabbed that opportunity hoping that there are just as many people like us who appreciate this longest-running version of the group.

CHARLES: **So you're not necessarily depicting the Silver Age versions as you are the classic versions of these characters.**

ALEX: Right. The story is not drawn or going to be looking in any way like it is set in the 1950s or '60s. Technically, within published history, the version of the group that you see here would have appeared between the years of 1960 and 1985 or so. That's not entirely correct, but you get the idea. The thing is, that doesn't matter. Thanks to other media, i.e.: the *Super Friends* cartoons, toys, and such, there's been a persistence of these particular characters. You know, the orange-shirted Aquaman and so on. Generally, the look of these guys as the primary components of the Justice League is something that's been carried through in all aspects of the various media incarnations that most people are aware of.

CHARLES: **When you speak about going back to the basics on these characters, going back to their original conceptions, why then are you not doing the original Flash and the original Green Lantern, Jay Garrick and Alan Scott?**

ALEX: To my mind—and again it gets to be very subjective if not entirely personal to say this—it's a division between what the Golden Age gave us in terms of an idea, versus what was refined ten or so years later. I believe that, to their credit, guys like Julius Schwartz and Gardner Fox took these earlier designs and reworked them in a way that made them stronger. If you think about the Silver Age costumes of the Flash and Green Lantern, which are the most dramatic revisions from their Golden Age counterparts, they became much more focused on who these characters were, and the potential that their very concepts held.

CHARLES: But couldn't it be said that today's readers feel the same way about Kyle Rayner?

ALEX: They very much can. It becomes an embrace of the age that you love the most. Basically, this is an opportunity for Paul and myself to do the versions of the characters that we appreciate the most.

CHARLES: So, in dedicating two years of your life to SECRET ORIGINS and LIBERTY AND JUSTICE, you have to make a choice about what excites you.

ALEX: Right. And a key thing about this, too, is that DC's been congenial enough to allow this book, which ultimately challenges continuity to a degree because the current continuity wiped out the published history of the League as we knew it.

CHARLES: This book being LIBERTY AND JUSTICE, you mean?

ALEX: Yes, LIBERTY AND JUSTICE. There is no historical Justice League in current continuity that would have allowed for Wonder Woman and Barry Allen to have been on the same team together.

JOEY CAVALIERI: Speaking of things you grew up with, can you speak a little bit to working in the tabloid format?

ALEX: Oh, yeah. Again, another thing that DC has been generous with has been to allow this indulgence of the tabloid format. We've been creating these oversized throwbacks to the '70s when, for a great period of time, there were—

CHARLES: Famous First Editions and all those Treasury Editions...

ALEX: ...and Collector's Editions, featuring great stories like SUPERMAN VS. SPIDER-MAN and SUPERMAN VS. MUHAMMAD ALI. Some of them were not original material but simply reprints. But they were what introduced another generation—my generation—to these characters and to the historical importance of some of their stories. These tabloids were an inexpensive format that a young kid could beg his parents to buy him for only a couple of bucks. They contained reprints of ACTION COMICS #1, or a collection of odd JLA stories, which is, again, my introduction to a lot of that classic material. I wouldn't have known what either the Golden Age or the Silver Age looked like without those reprints. I so loved that format because of the true grandeur that the work seemed to attain when it was printed at that size. Particularly when graphic artists like Neal Adams and say, Ross Andru and Dick Giordano, got a chance to work that large, they truly took advantage of the space to make their work seem that much more epic. Part of the aim of LIBERTY AND JUSTICE is to give people an even more epic feel than what we've done in our four previous graphic novels of Superman, Batman, Captain Marvel, and Wonder Woman. Paul and I are trying to create a more action-oriented comics story with a lot of vivid energy and motion between scenes, dialogue that's spoken in word balloons as well as captions, and much more heated moment-to-moment intercutting between the scenes. More panels. More depth. More drama.

CHARLES: When you were first conceptualizing this series, which began with PEACE ON EARTH, you chose that big format to allow you to do just that. To expand your storytelling and show your art in a way that would get attention for this series as well as attention for the characters.

ALEX: Right, the goal was for a much broader vision. You were getting bigger images spread over two pages. They were designed to be an easier read for a person who's not necessarily used to reading comics at all, either a child or an adult, without being confused. By eliminating all of the smaller panels, one is able to look at a double-page spread and immediately know how to read it. The comics language can, many times, be too much of a brick wall for people who didn't grow up reading it. I wanted to create a book that used very well-known characters that would actually reach out there and attract people who never read a comic before in their lives. They'd be able to read the text without trying to navigate the arrow-pointing of word balloons. They'd be able to fully appreciate some of the possibilities of the graphics of comics. Since I've done that now for four years, my feeling is maybe if that goal was reached, then that stuff is already out there for new readers. Now it's time for an action story. It's time to get back to what I was doing before, with works like KINGDOM COME and *Marvels*, and make better use of my skills as an action artist rather than an introspective artist.

JOEY: That's interesting, because a lot of the stuff that you do seems deliberately iconic. You seem to strive toward depicting *the* shot of the hero, or the shot that really defines the character.

ALEX: You will still get those kinds of glory shots. They just have to be planned out, with a greater purpose. In some ways, they're going to be compromising a certain amount of space. The heroes won't necessarily get a full double-page spread to gloryhog. Not each and every character. There's going to be some element of that but, for the greater satisfaction of being sucked into a story, you're going to get a lot more of like, "OK, we're in the thick of it, we're really feeling this thing going forward with a greater speed and momentum." And you'll feel it. As a kid, I'd dreamed—I mean, I literally had vivid dreams—of working on something this over the top. A single epic of the Justice League in an adventure that would completely captivate you. You know, it would take an entire evening to sit down and absorb the thing.

CHARLES: How else is JLA: LIBERTY AND JUSTICE different from the books that preceded it?

ALEX: LIBERTY AND JUSTICE is its own entity, separate from those other works. Even the cover we're planning is more in-your-face. Instead of just a big, stoic head shot, it's the group rushing at you, suggesting there's almost too much to contain what's inside.

CHARLES: In SECRET ORIGINS, you and Paul had to make certain choices in addition to deciding upon what versions of the characters to depict. One choice you faced concerned the moments from each origin that you were going to show. Another choice was the point of view that would be best to tell the stories from.

ALEX: This all goes back to 1997 when, before Paul Dini came on board the project, it was just me and you, Charlie, talking about wanting to pitch an oversized comic format for these four books. Each one of those tabloids would feature, at the outset, an origin of the character on a two-page spread. The inspiration for that came from the fact that the origins of Superman and Batman, by Siegel and Shuster and Kane originally, were done in these simple two-page formats when they first appeared back in 1939. Those creators did the very first origins we ever saw in comics. And they told these things simply, within two pages. Those moments have been reprinted a thousand times since. They became iconic through the simple graphics used—like the rocket coming from the exploding planet Krypton or, in Batman's case, his large looming head above his origin's beginning. That inspired me to mock up layouts of those two characters, and try to update their origins for a new age, to update it to where it worked within my painted graphics. I discovered I could tell the character's origin within nine panels: one large, wide panel across the top, eight smaller ones across the bottom. Within that format, I knew I was going to take Superman's origin and end on a glory shot of—"And here's Superman!"

CHARLES: You chose to do it monochromatically, too.

[ABOVE] PROMOTIONAL ART, SUPERMAN: PEACE ON EARTH, BATMAN: WAR ON CRIME, SHAZAM! POWER OF HOPE, AND WONDER WOMAN: SPIRIT OF TRUTH

[LEFT] PRELIMINARY PENCILS, JLA: LIBERTY AND JUSTICE

ALEX: I meant to invoke a sense of how this is a bygone age. That this is the past, this is a story that's legendary. So Superman had this very brown, earthy tone meant to invoke his very earthy origins. Despite the fact that he's from another planet, he's really this guy from the Midwestern United States. He's from the heartland, and I wanted you to feel that throughout the story. Of course, it's the opposite with Batman. I used a darker shade to color a much darker tale. At its core, what formed him is a story of great tragedy. With Batman's origin, I didn't want to follow the exact same model as Superman's. I didn't want to wind up with just—"Here's a glory shot of Batman at the end." To me, his origin had this special quality. It wasn't so much who he wound up as, it's the fact that a kid—well, imagine that a young boy makes a determination, "I'm going to grow up to be a fireman." Very few people will follow that through. Well, here's a kid who made a dedication to change his life. A one-man war on crime that would forever disturb and distort his adulthood. But he held to it. And he made this promise, he swore this oath when he was, like, eight. I thought, what a wonderful moment to end upon. So I wanted to actually tell Batman's origin backward, in a weird way. Going back and asking, "OK, this guy worked on his mind and body, but what was it that *caused* this?"

CHARLES: And Captain Marvel?

ALEX: Captain Marvel and Wonder Woman have never had their origins told in such shortened formats. When they came about in 1940, they both had multi-page origins. Wonder Woman especially had a wealth of information. So we had to solve the riddle: How do you refine and distill these other characters down to the same two-page format as Superman and Batman? In the end, as with a lot of things like this, it was a temptation to continue further and say, "Geez, that wasn't so hard. I bet we could do it with Aquaman and Flash and Green Lantern as well." So there was a greater desire to go and do that with the rest of the DC Universe. And that led to SECRET ORIGINS, where we're taking it to the fullest measure. Now the question I didn't answer that you brought up was about perspective.

CHARLES: Right. Each origin is told from a different point of view.

ALEX: Yeah, for Superman and Batman, we just used simple first-person perspective. For Superman, we adopted a very passionate tone. Very honest, straightforward, but like he's telling the greatest myth of all super hero myths. Which could almost be considered cornball to some degree, but there's such a direct honesty to it. There's no hint of irony or of a tongue-in-cheek quality to his beginnings, to what brings him to becoming this guy called Superman. But everybody else can't have that same earnestness in each and every origin. Therefore, we wanted to try something different creatively. Knowing two years ago when we were doing Captain Marvel that we might continue further, I always thought that if we got a chance to do some of these other characters, it would be cooler not to have every single one of them be first person.

CHARLES: For example, with Captain Marvel. You chose the Old Wizard's point of view. Same thing for Wonder Woman, which was from Hippolyta's point of view.

ALEX: I can't remember if that was Paul's idea. I know I pushed for Hippolyta because I wanted to give a contrast to the others. We couldn't just have one that wasn't told from the hero's point of view. For the other origins, it provided a model by which we had more latitude toward how we approached each character's perspective. Picking Iris Allen as the narrator of her husband/fiancé's origins seemed appropriate. Especially given the fact that the Flash was almost a new stage in super hero development. DC actually let a character become truly involved in an established real relationship—one that would lead to marriage. He may not have been the only one like that. There would also be the Atom and Hawkman and Aquaman. But I wanted to embrace that aspect of who he was, the idea that here's something that separates this guy from just being Joe Average. It was a depth that I wanted to instill into the character. That's why it didn't end up being, "I became the Flash, I did this, I did that."

CHARLES: What about the Atom?

ALEX: The Atom is a regular kind of guy. You get a sense of some of these heroes as people you can recognize. You know, it's not all just a big collection of aliens and football players or something. This is a collection of people from all different walks of life.

CHARLES: You individualized the heroes' experiences to make each special.

ALEX: Right. Like Aquaman. I enjoyed seeing his presence on the current *Justice League* cartoon show, which had that clear setup of him as a king, a husband, and a father. He was going to do everything for this new family, which included his kingdom. And that was represented as the truest defining thing

about this great hero. That makes him so different than anybody else. No one else in this grouping is a ruler. No one else in this grouping is a father, either. So Paul and I thought that was something to emphasize. That's why his origin went the way that it did. We could've not acknowledged that he had a son. We could have just skipped by that. But given the timing of when this story could arguably be taking place, we can pretty much put him at this sort of perfect point in his life when he had Mera and Arthur Jr. and Aqualad and all these things that we think of as classic Aquaman.

JOEY: More than that, they are things you need to know about the character to appreciate another adventure featuring him. That's part of what you try to work into an origin even in a regular comic book.

ALEX: The best you can hope for, of course, is that you give people enough elements to say, "Oh, I like this guy now. I've been given enough information in both text and visuals to appreciate him. I can see that the Flash and the Atom are not alike." Or, "I can see that this guy has more to offer than this other super hero."

JOEY: What else would you like people to take away from the book? Not just SECRET ORIGINS, but LIBERTY AND JUSTICE as well?

ALEX: I think part of the reason this project exists with DC's characters is that DC truly has legendary iconic heroes that the world knows. Even though competing companies may be reaching out there with strong, popular characters, there's nothing that really compares with the near-Olympic myth that the DC pantheon achieves. When you put Superman with Batman and Wonder Woman together, you get this lineup of the world's greatest legends. In terms of super heroes, these are the first names that everyone knows. You'll find that most other heroes start much further down the line in the public's consciousness. No matter how popular other super heroes have become in recent years, the world still knows DC's characters first.

JOEY: They're the archetypes.

ALEX: They're the prototypes for what has been copied time and time again with other comic book companies. Pretty much everything spins from Superman to some degree as the first super hero. And without Wonder Woman to precede all female super heroes, you wouldn't have had any of them. These guys are the precedents for everything. First those big three. Then other concepts that subsequently came out of DC still retained a lot of that epic quality. Even somebody like Green Arrow was himself just a Batman copycat for many years until he truly came into his own and became a legend, and an influential force within the history of comics. These guys are the greats.

I don't mind revisions, because these are continually self-renewing legends. Superman is currently on TV with *Smallville*, being reintroduced to the world every week with a new adventure of himself as a teenager. Arguably, that's what can always be done with these icons. They can always be rejuvenated. It's my belief as a fan that this is a key to what makes DC's characters strong. That's where you get into a bit of a debate. Fans can argue whether you can do that with many second-string characters, but when you start doing it with somebody like Batman—which has already been attempted—does it really work? We've seen it done before: We've seen *Batman Beyond*. We've seen ten years ago when they replaced Batman for a period of time with stand-ins like Azrael.

JOEY: Well, *Batman Beyond* still has Bruce.

CHARLES: Yeah, it's an extension of who the character is, it just contains an addition. It's not a replication or a replacement.

ALEX: The reason that never came off as a bad thing is because it was never offered as a replacement. There may be several revisions going into the future. Someday maybe it will be Atom Man or Dr. Nightmare that are the lead characters in Justice League. But ultimately, we are using the key heroes, not so much because they are in the JLA, but because they are *the* icons. This is DC's foremost grouping. JLA isn't just some group that DC publishes. JLA is a lineup of DC's greatest legends.

CHARLES: Why didn't you choose to depict certain aspects of the characters that everyone remembers, like the Flash's costume coming out of his ring?

[RIGHT] PRELIMINARY PENCILS FOR COVER, JLA: LIBERTY AND JUSTICE
[LEFT, TOP] PRELIMINARY PENCILS FOR COVER, JLA: SECRET ORIGINS
[LEFT, BOTTOM] PRELIMINARY PENCILS FOR COVER, JLA: SECRET ORIGINS

ALEX: I'm trying to embrace details about the characters that seem to stand the test of time fairly well, and gloss over the things that might seem a little dated. There are things that we've always enjoyed about these characters: the fact that Green Lantern's ring never worked on anything yellow. Well, that was fun for a lot of more innocently written material, but when you try to take it seriously...that's usually a problem that always happens with all of my books. The realistic way they look demands that they have a serious tone to them. So we're not embracing things like the costume that comes out of the tiny ring, even though most old fanboys, we love stuff like that.

Here's another interesting example, taken from the origins. If you look at certain moments in the characters' history, some of these things that I represented as a single panel were expanded adventures that may not stand the test of time. For Aquaman, when you see his wedding, you've got Aqualad there, the old Robin, and the whole Justice League wearing fish helmets on their heads. In the context of how we presented it, it seems like a serious enough moment. But if you try to examine that too realistically, it begins to break apart.

In the LIBERTY AND JUSTICE book, we're planning on acknowledging some of the JLA's greatest battles, some of the more fun but not-so-believable adventures or villains that the JLA may have been up against. But the version of them that Paul and I present to you is only going to seem more credible. I don't necessarily care for redefining the past and deciding, "This guy was just way too corny, so now I'm going to redo Kanjar Ro so he's completely the coolest villain you've ever seen." I'd rather, if we need to acknowledge anything from the past, just gloss over it lightly or direct the eye toward something that seems stronger, but not completely ignore or redefine. Nothing that we've done in SECRET ORIGINS actually contradicts published history.

CHARLES: So, you're not throwing things out, so much as you're just not dealing with them directly.

ALEX: Exactly. Here's a good example: In the origin of Superman, you see Krypton exploding. You see a rocket-shaped vehicle coming toward us, but you don't see the exact configuration of the vehicle. So for all you know, it could be the one from the 1986 John Byrne version of Superman, or it could be the one from the 1939 origin, which has a more "Flash Gordon" style rocket. I never show you the vehicle, so I'm not actually dating the project. I'm not redefining the past. The thing that's drawn in SECRET ORIGINS looks like it could have been from any version of the origin.

JOEY: I think that some people might find that exclusive, but I find it inclusive. Anybody who's ever read a Superman comic at any time can look at that and say, "Yeah, that's what I remember."

ALEX: To begin with the destruction of Krypton, you acknowledge that this is a kid who was rescued by whoever lived on Krypton. He's the sole survivor. That's all you need to know. Just like on the *Smallville* television show. They still haven't gotten into who his birth parents were, or where he came from. All you need to know is that he was saved. Somebody saved this little kid. And that's what matters. You don't need to know what particular clothing Jor-El wore. The minute you start losing time to focus on those kinds of elements, you begin to sort of get into a war between your fan bases. So the way of doing these spreads in SECRET ORIGINS was meant to make it kind of a level playing field for everybody. Classic enough for the old fans like myself, yet it's believable and strong enough for the cynical age we're in today.

CHARLES: So these are the kinds of things you and Paul work out in advance. Why don't you describe how the two of you work together?

ALEX: On all four books before this, we had lengthy conversations that would lead to Paul writing an outline. However, for SUPERMAN: PEACE ON EARTH, I had written an initial treatment of what my thoughts would be on the story. I wrote about eight pages of handwritten notes to describe everything I wanted in there.

CHARLES: You wrote that treatment because originally you were going to write that book.

ALEX: That was the plan. I thought, maybe I could write as well as illustrate it. But I didn't have the absolute self-confidence that one would need to complete not just one book, but all four. I knew that if I had somebody to collaborate with, I could comfortably get all of the ideas I wanted in there and also build off of what they brought to the project as well. Then I could get the book *done*, as opposed to wasting many more months staring at a blank sheet of paper trying to write something. Not that I would have stared; I just would have written something really bad on that blank sheet of paper. [*Laughter*] You get the idea.

So Paul came to my rescue by being willing to do it at the time. I was a fan of his, and he apparently appreciated my work. It was a real surprise and a feeling of great fortune that I could get a well-regarded, Emmy Award-winning writer to work with me on this. From that point forward, it had always been "conversation-conversation-outline," and then I would take the outline and physically break it down into the number of panels necessary to tell that story. This is the way that comics had been done a number of times before, where the initial thing that's offered to the artist is just a simple outline. The artist would then have to break down the action into a number of panels. Next, the writer would have to come in and provide text on top of that. But because this was not going to be a story with dialogue but blocks of copy instead, it was easier to let me have latitude, because the text over my visuals would be a much more stream-of-consciousness voice from a narrator. It became a very easy way to grow my ability to lay out a subject carefully enough to know how many panels it was going to take to really move us through a scene. And I wasn't really at this point in my storytelling ability before then. But, you know, I learned how to do it better through the course of this. So that now, when we did SECRET ORIGINS, I pretty much sat down after having my initial conversations with Paul to get a sense of, you know, did he have any ideas? Did he have a perspective he wanted to try on a character besides just sort of going through the published historical origins and really editing them down? Because our job was, more than anything else, an editing process of compressing a great deal of information into nine panels.

JOEY: A kind of shorthand.

ALEX: Yeah. Just to try to combine the kinds of things that would seem to have the right kind of gravity to them. I mean, a lot of the images that you see me pick weren't ones that were the grandiose images that were presented to me. Like a shot of Aquaman standing in front of Atlantis. That's not based upon one image or one era. It was just instinct taking me to that. On the other hand, the shot of the Flash running across the street in the top panel of his origin was influenced by the first page of his SHOWCASE debut, where he runs along at full speed. I thought, "*That's* the kind of image you want to open on! That's what you need to say about the Flash!" Because it's all about taking advantage of that wide, expansive space, with multiple shots of the figure running and all that kind of stuff. With Green Lantern, it was more about what he was a part of, the great lineage of so many Green Lanterns across the universe.

JOEY: Well, this is a preview, so maybe you should talk a little bit about the broad story of LIBERTY AND JUSTICE.

[ABOVE] PRELIMINARY PENCILS FOR PROMOTIONAL POSTER, JLA: LIBERTY AND JUSTICE
[RIGHT] PRELIMINARY PENCILS, JLA: SECRET ORIGINS

ALEX: The threat in LIBERTY AND JUSTICE is of extraterrestrial origin. That's something that typifies most Justice League stories. Most all of them deal with, "Here's your villain from planet Pluto." It's always something outside the norm. Instead, we're trying to make it a reasonable representation of the world and depict the antagonist in our tale as the most realistic form of "JLA villain" that we could think of. So we have a lot of interplay between the Justice League and regular people.

In some ways, this adventure has great elements to it that, to me, are nostalgic. They're things I enjoyed in JUSTICE LEAGUE comics when I was a kid. A moment here, a moment there. Like, there's a favorite story of mine called "Takeover of the Earth Masters," which came out in 1975, I believe. It was the very first JUSTICE LEAGUE comic I ever got. It was a two-part adventure that had a ... well, I won't describe what it had, in case any fans go back and say, "Hey, maybe this is what they're doing!" But it wouldn't be bad to mention the comic as an influence on me. Pretty much anything I was influenced by in all the comics I read as a kid, I am trying to inject into this. As well as ideas for new graphics for some of the characters. For instance, I'm trying to make Aquaman into a real tough character. I want to make people respect every member of this team.

The presence of characters like Superman, Batman, and Wonder Woman can't be avoided, and they're made use of in this. However, we really try to spotlight many of DC's secondary icons. I hope that this book will add to their legend and give them broad exposure. One of the greatest things about the oversized tabloid books is that, as they go straight to comic book stores, they also go straight to bookstores across the U.S. and eventually throughout the world.

CHARLES: That was the goal when this series was first conceived. You and I felt that if we released another standard-sized comic into the marketplace, we wouldn't get the bookstore placement or review attention that we ultimately did. The format is saying, "This series of books is different from everything else. We want you to pay attention to it."

ALEX: I've been really grateful that I can go into a bookstore and see Wonder Woman or Batman poking above a shelf and know that just the title of those books alone—even if nothing else is showing—is rising above everything else around it. That can't be denied as an influential thing in getting this out there.

CHARLES: So what's next for you guys?

ALEX: What's next? [*Laughter*] Haven't I done enough for you people? Dear God, I'm going to be working on this for the next *year*!

JOEY: You know, you said that five years ago! [*Laughter*]

[ABOVE AND RIGHT] PRELIMINARY PENCILS, JLA: LIBERTY AND JUSTICE

[TOP] LITHOGRAPH, "THE ORIGINAL SEVEN," (THE WARNER BROS. STUDIO STORE GALLERY, 2001)

"OK, you've seen the four major guys, now here's everybody else to top it all off."
—PAUL DINI

INTERVIEW WITH PAUL DINI, THURSDAY, OCTOBER 3, 2002

CHARLES KOCHMAN: **Let's start at the top—the dedication. Why Gardner Fox and Julie Schwartz?**

PAUL DINI: We really look upon them as the guys who kept the light of DC Comics burning from the Golden Age into the Silver Age by keeping the characters going, and then combining some of the key characters into the group that became the Justice League in THE BRAVE AND THE BOLD. Also, Gardner Fox wrote a ton of those stories. It was not an easy juggling feat to keep all of those characters in play in one story. You've got to admire the man for that. In Julie's case in particular, his enthusiasm for the characters kept them alive and also kept the idea of them banded together as a team for a long time. Without these two guys, it wouldn't have gotten done.

CHARLES: **When you say it wouldn't have gotten done, just to clarify that, you mean the Justice League/Secret Origins kind of stuff?**

PAUL: I'm not a historian, but it seemed to me, looking back on those early stories, that Julie and Fox were mostly responsible for them, or responsible in a key way with the artists they were working with. Also, I think it's recognition long overdue, as much as we can give it, for Julie, who's been a terrific editor for all these years—he maintained a vision of these characters—and recognition for Fox, who added so much to the DC mythos and combined it into a whole universe in the early '60s, one that is still in effect today.

CHARLES: **I mentioned the dedication to Julie in the hallway the other day. He was flattered.**

PAUL: Oh, that's sweet. I'm glad he liked it. We're happy to do it.

CHARLES: **In terms of you and Alex working together, why don't you talk about how that collaboration works? What's the process like?**

PAUL: Usually, we start with a rough idea of what we're going to do by working out our take on a given character. Alex is very dedicated to the primary versions of each of the DC super heroes we've done so far in these books. So, rather than telling the ultimate Superman story or ultimate Wonder Woman story and making them the greatest Superman-saves-the-world or Wonder-Woman-fights-the-gods-of-Olympus stories, Alex likes to return it to whatever the character is at his or her original core. To go back to the spirit of the character and not necessarily tell the big story-to-end-all-stories. At the beginning, we decided that we were going to tell *a* story about each character that would remind both fans and casual readers just who these heroes were. So that you would see Superman's devotion to mankind and how he struggles to do something out of his heart for the betterment of humanity. Batman, we showed him as very driven: a man obsessed with his parents' death, who in some ways imagines himself as sort of dead. He had embarked on this big campaign against crime and is now just driven by the need to punish the offenders. With these stories, it wasn't the big ultimate super hero story, it was just the one that told you who they were and re-emphasized that. Once we started with that point of view, then the rest of the plot took shape around that original idea. We would go back and forth and talk out ideas and situations that showed the characters at their best, doing what they do best.

When we were first plotting these out, we would meet in person every year, usually in the fall, either socially or when we were doing a signing, and schedule a night or two to map out whatever it was the next book would be. Just get a little face time in and talk it out between us. Then a series of phone calls would take place, and then we would talk to you guys, our editors at DC Comics, about where we wanted to go with the story. Alex would begin sketching up some ideas that I would see. Then I, in turn, would write a fairly detailed outline based upon what we were talking about. Then Alex would sketch some thumbnails of the story's action. I would then proceed to write a more detailed outline from which Alex would basically break down the whole book. It's very kinetic—I would write responding to his drawings, and if I came up with ideas that he responded to, then I would work them up more in the outline. So we'd go back and forth on it. It's kind of hard to work that way, over 2,000 miles apart, but over time, it did evolve into a working system. It wasn't a situation where I would just write a script and Alex would draw it. We

wanted to keep the ideas fresh and we wanted to keep the door open so that if one of us had another idea, we'd call up the other one and say, "How about we put this in?" Or, "Here's a story beat I want to concentrate on." Or, "We need some more action here. Let's talk about where we can send Captain Marvel in the middle of this adventure so that we can play up what he's doing with these kids in the story, but also get a beat of action in there." We'd wrestle with it over a period of time and it would work out great.

CHARLES: **Over the past four years, you tackled the four major icons—Superman, Batman, Captain Marvel, and Wonder Woman. Now, your latest project is JLA: SECRET ORIGINS, the prequel to the upcoming extravaganza JLA: LIBERTY AND JUSTICE. How did these two projects come into being?**

PAUL: Alex and I had talked rather informally about a big project to cap off the four previous tabloid books, and we thought the only thing big enough was a story that would combine most of the characters we'd seen before, and also bring in the rest of the major players in the DC Universe. And what better story to concentrate on than a Justice League story? Because most of the key DC characters have also been members, either through direct association, or else through casual association, with the Justice League. And we thought, this is a chance to not only do the four major heroes we've done before, but a chance to work in many of the classic supporting characters, characters that the fans love and that we love. We knew we might never have a chance to work on a big Flash book or a big Aquaman book or Green Arrow. However, if we did a Justice League book, we could put them all in there and have an opportunity to find fun story beats for all of them. It was really a way of saying, "OK, you've seen the four major guys, now here's everybody else with a great big story to top it all off." In discussing this with DC, you guys thought, "Hey, wouldn't it be great to do a little prequel to get people excited about it?" And now here we are.

JOEY CAVALIERI: **If it were totally up to you and you could do a book on any one of the characters in SECRET ORIGINS, which one would you**

[ABOVE] PRELIMINARY PENCILS FOR PROMOTIONAL POSTER, JLA: LIBERTY AND JUSTICE
[RIGHT] PRELIMINARY PENCILS, JLA: SECRET ORIGINS

pick? Do you have a favorite among them?

PAUL: Of all the characters that we've highlighted in the book? It's funny. Last year, I had written, with Warner Bros. co-producer Alan Burnett, a currently unscheduled Batman direct-to-video that featured Green Arrow and Plastic Man. As a writer, it was fun finding a "voice" for them in the script, and just as much fun working with them in SECRET ORIGINS. As a kid, I loved the old cartoons of Aquaman riding around on a sea horse. Being the king under the sea, I thought there was something cool about that. It was a fond memory to look back and see him and say, "Hey, there he is riding the old sea horse. There he is with Mera and his family." If I had to pick one, I might pick one of those guys. Once you get into those characters, I think you're dealing more in the realms of action and fantasy than with the others, because I don't think they're as primal or as primary as Batman, Superman, and Wonder Woman. You're looking at other elements that tell the story with them, whereas you *can* tell "real-world" stories with Batman and Superman. Once you begin telling stories with the Atom, if he's not going to be shrinking down and going to subatomic worlds, there's sort of no point in doing him. Likewise Aquaman—it's all under the water and so you're dealing with much more "larger-than-life," fantastic threats. Not to demean those characters in any way. It's just that once you've established Superman and Batman, and how they're sort of polar opposites in what they mean to mankind, then you start dealing more with characters that have more colorful powers. And that gets to be more about the power and the character's world than about what a hero like Green Lantern means to mankind. It's more about fighting aliens and being a part of a league of interstellar peacekeepers.

JOEY: **Do you have a favorite of the four you've done previously?**

PAUL: I really have a fondness for SHAZAM! POWER OF HOPE. I think that's just because it seemed a little bit lighter than the others and a little more heartfelt, perhaps because of the fact that deep down Captain Marvel is a child posing as an adult who's doing things for kids. It's a sentimental favorite. There's just some very cool stuff in it with him being the big hero to the kids. He's taking them on adventures, but also occasionally getting into trouble and then having to be both a responsible adult, yet really the kid at heart who takes kind of a kid-like attitude toward saving people and effecting rescues. So I've always found that juxtaposition a lot of fun with Captain Marvel.

CHARLES: **Let's get back to SECRET ORIGINS for a second. In doing this book, you guys had to pick a certain lineup, certain versions of the characters, like Hal Jordan or Barry Allen, versus Kyle Rayner or Wally West. How did you and Alex arrive at what versions of the classic super heroes you wanted to do?**

PAUL: Well, this is by no means a slap at any of the creators who have come after the Silver Age of comics, which is the late '50s to, I believe, the early '70s. I'm a fan of a lot of the books that came after, and I certainly enjoy those interpretations of the characters. It's just that with every one of the books we've done before, we went back to the core versions of the original characters, and we thought, with JUSTICE LEAGUE, let's do the same thing. That, even though a big part of our fan base was not even alive when this version of the Justice League was around, it is still the version we feel a lot of people remember. Those versions of the characters are very archetypal. Those were the ones that we wanted to concentrate on the most. In our minds, this was the version we read when we were growing up, or that we knew in different forms throughout our childhood, so we wanted to go back and revisit that. Like, there's the Green Lantern: You don't need to know an awful lot about his background, but he is kinda the guy you remember seeing all those years. There's the Atom: You kind of remember the broad strokes on him. Or the Flash, also.

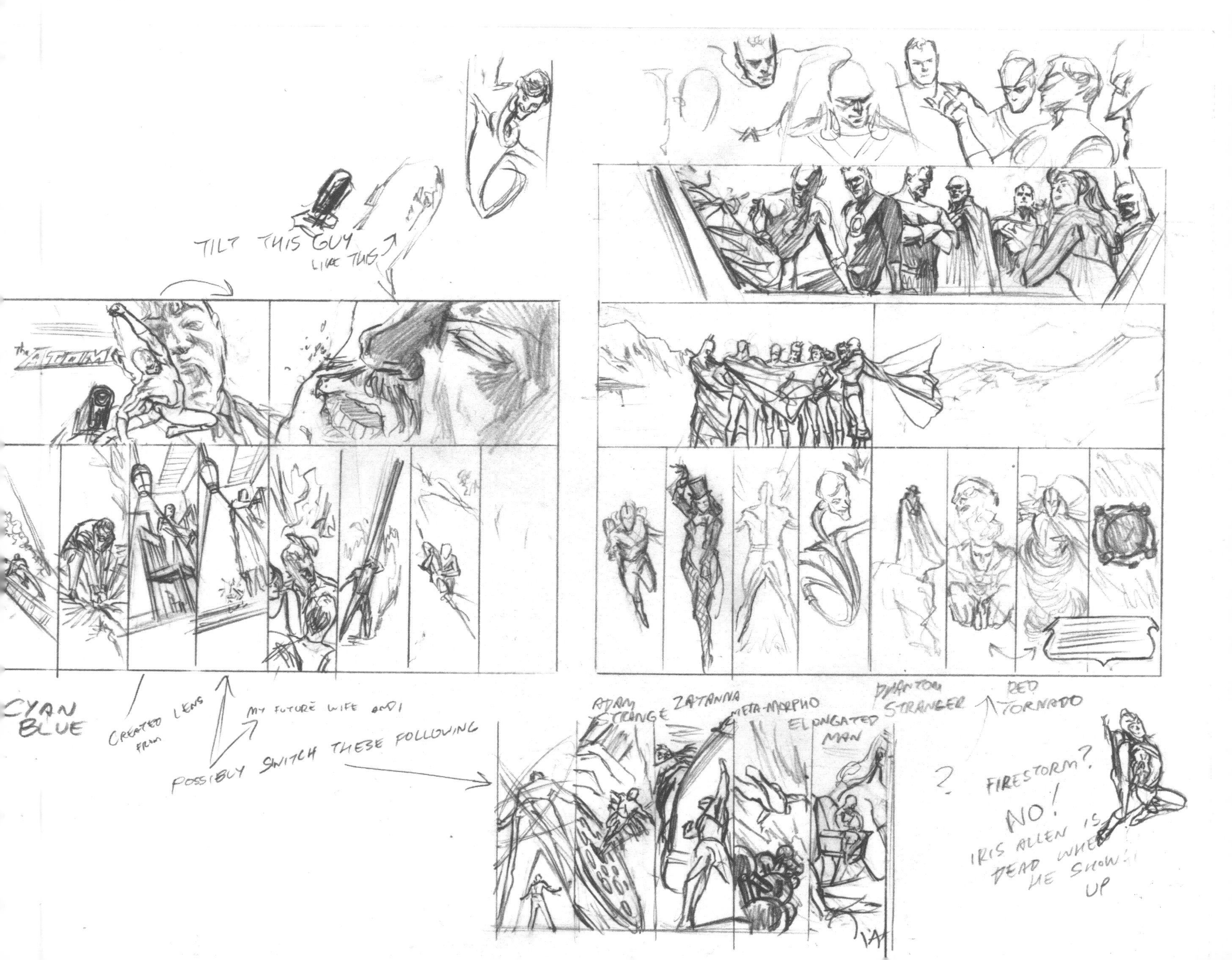

So not only are the characters' alter egos the classic versions, but the heroes themselves are being looked at in that same kind of primary light. It was easier to do it that way. It was a sentimental choice more than anything. I'm very happy that we made it, as I have a lot of affection for those characters. When I think of the Justice League as a team, I always think of those basic guys.

CHARLES: **For the origin spreads, you said you were trying to find aspects of their origins that have always been there, but not fully explored, and a perspective on each one that makes them unique. Want to talk more about that?**

PAUL: To a great degree, we did a fair number from the point of view of the hero telling his own origin story. But we also wanted to shake it up and give other people's perspective on the heroes, so that it wasn't just, "I'm so-and-so and here's how I got my powers."

CHARLES: **When we initially spoke about this, I remember you said you wanted to generate a surprise factor in the reading of each individual origin, so that by the time readers got to the end of the spread, they would have an epiphany on the point of view. They would read along, and it wouldn't be until the end where they would have to go back and say, "Oh, I see what's going on." I'm sure that's been the challenge you faced in writing these.**

PAUL: Absolutely—and that was definitely the case in, say, the Aquaman spread, because with him I thought it might be rather dull if he talked about himself: "I was a lost baby from Atlantis." We thought, as long as he's got this mythic quality of being the undersea king, why not have his origin told more in the form of a legend? Not told specifically by one person, but as if it's echoed throughout the ocean by his people and the sea creatures. If the final image is Aquaman and his family standing in front of the Atlanteans revering him as their king, and him waving to them, then what better point of view for the story to be told than by his people and told in a style that befits a legendary monarch like a King Arthur? Certainly his legend would be told in that form, rather than he, as a king, telling it himself.

With the Flash, because Iris—Barry Allen's fiancée—was such a key part of the early stories, we thought it would be fun to let it be from her perspective. Early on, Barry Allen was a police scientist who was always obsessed with doing his job. He was diligent, but he was also very slow, so who better to tell his story than the woman he was constantly standing up because he was being too methodical and too slow? Suddenly, he finds his life accelerated, so it's his fiancée's take on him and his powers, which I thought was pretty funny.

CHARLES: **Green Lantern's origin was pretty dramatic.**

PAUL: Again, we wanted to do something that talked about the majesty and commitment of the Green Lantern Corps and what it means to the universe. And since Hal Jordan is always sort of the everyman from Earth swept up into that situation, he naturally would have, I think, a more downbeat take on it. But we wanted something grander for that, so we gave the origin to Abin Sur, the alien who bequeaths him the ring and power upon his dying.

CHARLES: **He's also speaking from the dead.**

PAUL: That was a nod to the tone of a movie like *Sunset Boulevard*, which opens with the main character dead and floating in a pool. It's the same thing: Abin Sur is dead and propped up in Hal Jordan's arms, yet he's saying that the greatest feat he ever did as a Green Lantern was to pass his ring on to a worthy successor. So we thought a voice from beyond the grave was more than appropriate.

CHARLES: **You also had a lot of fun with Plastic Man.**

PAUL: I did. I wanted him to say in so many words, "I'm Plastic Man and I don't take anything seriously." He does a mock version of his origin which is a fun parody of Superman's. Then he goes into the spiel of who he was, this Eel O'Brian, a gangster who was kind of a bottom feeder, who got a second chance when he attained these amazing stretching powers. He talks about how that changed his whole life. It was all about change and kind of bouncing from one idea to another, just as Plastic Man always changes his body and always goes bouncing from one situation to another. That was a lot of fun for me to look at, because Alex has such a realistic approach to all his artwork. It was amazing to see him do the old Jack Cole images from the original origin. I knew he would pull it off in a very fun way. The sight of Plastic Man stretching his face and doing the transformations and everything...I thought it was wonderful to see Alex tackle that.

Hawkman, I always think of as a by-the-book guy; he comes from an advanced society where he was one of the key peacekeepers. Now he's come to Earth, doing more of the same thing. That origin was from his point of view as a stern lawman, yet different from Batman. Here's a guy who's very devoted to duty, yet very devoted to his wife as well. I was hoping to go for a feeling that would show both sides of his personality.

Atom was fun because you're putting him in a fantastic world with his ability to shrink. It's about "the little man" who was given these powers, so there were references to that throughout his origin, as in, "Don't ever count out the little guy." I liked the image of him shoulder-to-shoulder with the Justice League. He's literally almost on their shoulders rather than just standing beside them.

As for Green Arrow, I've always thought of Oliver Queen as kind of the wiseguy of the group. The tone of his first-person narration was rather sarcastic. It harkened back to what I always imagined that character to be like. Kind of brusque, kind of cynical, yet it shows his commitment to sticking up for the downtrodden in a Robin Hood kind of way. I looked at every take on Green Arrow back from the Denny O'Neil/Neal Adams incarnation right up to the Kevin Smith version, and that attitude is a central part of his character. I tried to echo that as best I could in my writing.

Martian Manhunter's origin spread, in many ways, sets the tone for LIBERTY AND JUSTICE because, I think, he lends a real common-man point of view to start off the new book. He's an alien stranded on Earth, much more alien than Superman. Superman doesn't have that many—if any—conscious memories of Krypton. I think they all came to him later through what he was told by his adoptive parents and what he discovered in his subsequent explorations of space and the history of Krypton. J'onn J'onzz lived on Mars. He saw his world die, he saw the people closest to him die, and he was basically rescued from that world as the last surviving Martian. So here's somebody who really knows what it's like to experience firsthand the loss not only of his family, but his entire planet. He's come to Earth and he has the power to blend in among mankind but, to a great degree as much as he looks human, he's always going to be one step removed from humanity. Yet, he has a commitment to use his powers to preserve our planet. The last thing he wants to see is another world die. Especially when he has the power to join other beings with similar abilities and safeguard the world and its people. J'onn can basically look like anybody and blend in with other people and get a sense of how they feel and how they live. Being a telepath, he realizes what goes through their minds. So there's a certain distance with him—he'll always have that by the nature of being a Martian—but there's also a tremendous amount of empathy with the character, because he does care for his adopted home and the Earth people and his teammates in the Justice League very much. In a way,

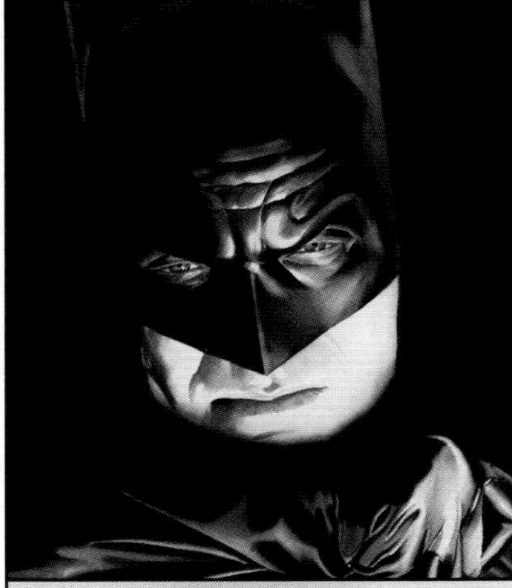

[ABOVE] COVER ART, SUPERMAN: PEACE ON EARTH, BATMAN: WAR ON CRIME, SHAZAM! POWER OF HOPE, AND WONDER WOMAN: SPIRIT OF TRUTH

[RIGHT] PRELIMINARY PENCILS, JLA: LIBERTY AND JUSTICE

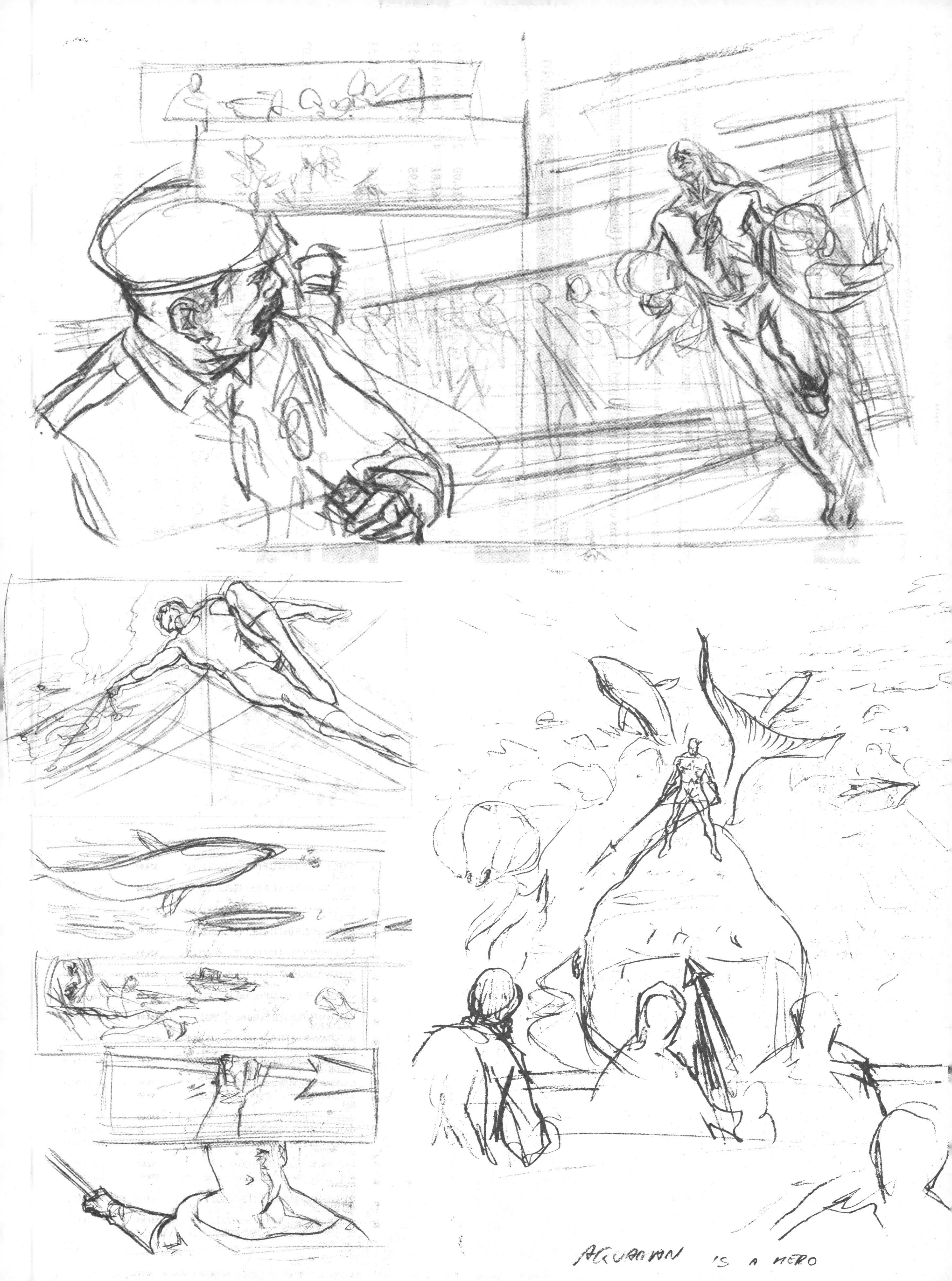
AQUAMAN IS A HERO

it makes him really the heart of that group of characters.

Still, I think a lot of LIBERTY AND JUSTICE is much more of an external story than an internal story. For the most part, the JLA are dealing with a situation that is a threat to mankind, and it's all about how they work together to stop that. When you've got so many characters interacting, it doesn't make sense to have the entire thing be an inner monologue from the point of view of one character. Besides, we're going to have anywhere from between sixteen and twenty DC players involved in the story, so let's have them all interacting and doing what they do best. Let's see some sparks fly when things get a little tense between the characters. Let's hear them talking, so to speak, and leave ourselves the option of having the action take over for several pages at a time as they go off to combat a different threat.

CHARLES: **So this book is going to have word balloons and more of the conventions of regular comic book storytelling?**

PAUL: Right. There'll be word balloons and character interaction. But there will still be some narrative text, used as we've done before, as well as traditional panel-to-panel sequencing.

JOEY: **Can you say something about the response you've gotten from the previous books?**

PAUL: I'd say pretty much overall the response has been very, very positive. In fact, almost unanimously so. As I said, they're not the be-all-end-all of super hero stories. It's not like Frank Miller's THE DARK KNIGHT RETURNS, which is the one great apocalyptic story about Batman. These are closer to stories that you can sit and read and maybe think about a little bit. And they're great stories for children. Every time I've read one to kids, they've really gotten into it. They might have seen heroes in fancy suits, but they never really knew that much about them. So this series is a good way to kind of refresh readers on who the characters are. Most of the people who have talked to me about them have always appreciated that factor. Here's the character, done right, and in a situation that the reader can relate to and, perhaps, be a little inspired by. I mean, there's been some quibbling here and there. You know, reviews where people have not liked a particular story or fans complained, for example, "Why'd they have to take Wonder Woman out of her costume? You've totally denied who she is and you've reduced her to nothing!" No—this is really not a story about her parading around as Princess of the Amazons. I mean, look at the way Alex paints! He's rendering what looks like a real woman in real-world situations. At some point, it stretches credibility to have her running around in her battle armor while meeting with world leaders. I felt we had to put her cape on and tone her down a little bit (this made her look more like an ambassador, which is what she is). By the end she realizes that she lives in the real world, the real *human* world of men and women, of ideals and reality, and she can do just as effective a job in real clothes as in the costume. That story is almost an allegory for the way super heroes are perceived and how they do their jobs. That's sort of allegorical for these books, too; by attempting a more realistic spin, we get a more realistic result. For instance, it would not do to have the PEACE ON EARTH story with Superman take place and suddenly Bizarro and Mr. Mxyzptlk and Luthor show up in the middle of it to cause trouble. It's the real world, Superman's dealing with a real situation, and guess what? He fails at it. But by his failure he gets a sort of epiphany of how to really help people. And it's not necessarily by trying to fulfill their wishes in an immediate and tangible form. It's working with mankind as one of them and through education—education is the first step in getting people to think for themselves.

CHARLES: **It's not a failure so much as he realizes he can't solve the world's problems; he has to lead by example. Less a failure than a self-realization, and then figuring out how to refocus who he is so that he can effect the greatest change.**

PAUL: Yep—Superman may be an alien, but he's human, too.

CHARLES: **So what's next?**

PAUL: [*Laughter*] I think it's time for a break. I love working with Alex and hope to always do so, but after JUSTICE LEAGUE, I think that's pretty much the capper on everything that we've done so far. If we never do another project like this, JLA is a nice hail and farewell to the DC Universe. It gave us a chance to work with all our favorite characters. Who knows? In eighteen months, Alex may call me up and say [*imitating Alex's voice*] "Hey, Paul, I've been thinking about it ... I've been thinking about the Wonder Twins, and there's a way it could work." [*Laughter*] Then I'll be like [*shouting over pretend cell phone static*], "Alex, I'm going through a tunnel! You're breaking up!" And then I run for the hills. If we're not going to do BLACK CANARY/ZATANNA: POWER OF FISHNETS, then I'm certainly not going to do a book on the Wonder Twins!

[LEFT] PRELIMINARY PENCILS FOR COVER, JLA: LIBERTY AND JUSTICE

[RIGHT] PRELIMINARY PENCILS FOR COVER OF PROPOSED OMNIBUS COLLECTION OF SUPERMAN: PEACE ON EARTH, BATMAN: WAR ON CRIME, SHAZAM! POWER OF HOPE, AND WONDER WOMAN: SPIRIT OF TRUTH

PAUL DINI is an Emmy Award-winning writer and producer (*The New Batman/Superman Adventures* and *Batman Beyond*). In comics he is the author of *Batman: Mad Love, Batman: Harley Quinn, Superman: Peace on Earth, Batman: War on Crime, Shazam! Power of Hope, Wonder Woman: Spirit of Truth,* and his creator-owned series *Jingle Belle* and *Mutant, Texas*. Dini has also collaborated with designer Chip Kidd on *Batman Animated* for HarperCollins, documenting the creation and unique visual styling of the groundbreaking TV series. Paul Dini lives in Los Angeles and is currently at work on a number of television, movie, and comics-related projects.

About the Authors

ALEX ROSS studied illustration at the American Academy of Art in Chicago, then honed his craft as a storyboard artist before entering the comics field. His miniseries *Marvels* (Marvel Comics, 1993) opened a wider acceptance for painted comics. He moved on to produce the equally successful *Kingdom Come* (DC Comics, 1996). Receiving critical acclaim and multiple awards for these best-selling works, Ross made a name as both an artist and storyteller, dedicating himself to bold experiments within the comics medium. Most recently, with the miniseries *Uncle Sam* (Vertigo/DC Comics, 1997), *Earth X* (Marvel Comics, 1999), *Universe X* (Marvel Comics, 2001), and the graphic novels *Superman: Peace on Earth* (DC Comics, 1998), *Batman: War on Crime* (DC Comics, 1999), *Shazam! Power of Hope* (DC Comics, 2000), and *Wonder Woman: Spirit of Truth* (DC Comics, 2001), he continues to bring comics to a broader audience. Alex Ross lives in Illinois.

DC COMICS

JLA: SECRET ORGINS. November, 2002. Published by DC Comics, 1700 Broadway, New York, NY 10019.

Printed in Canada. Second Printing.
DC Comics, A Warner Bros. Entertainment Company